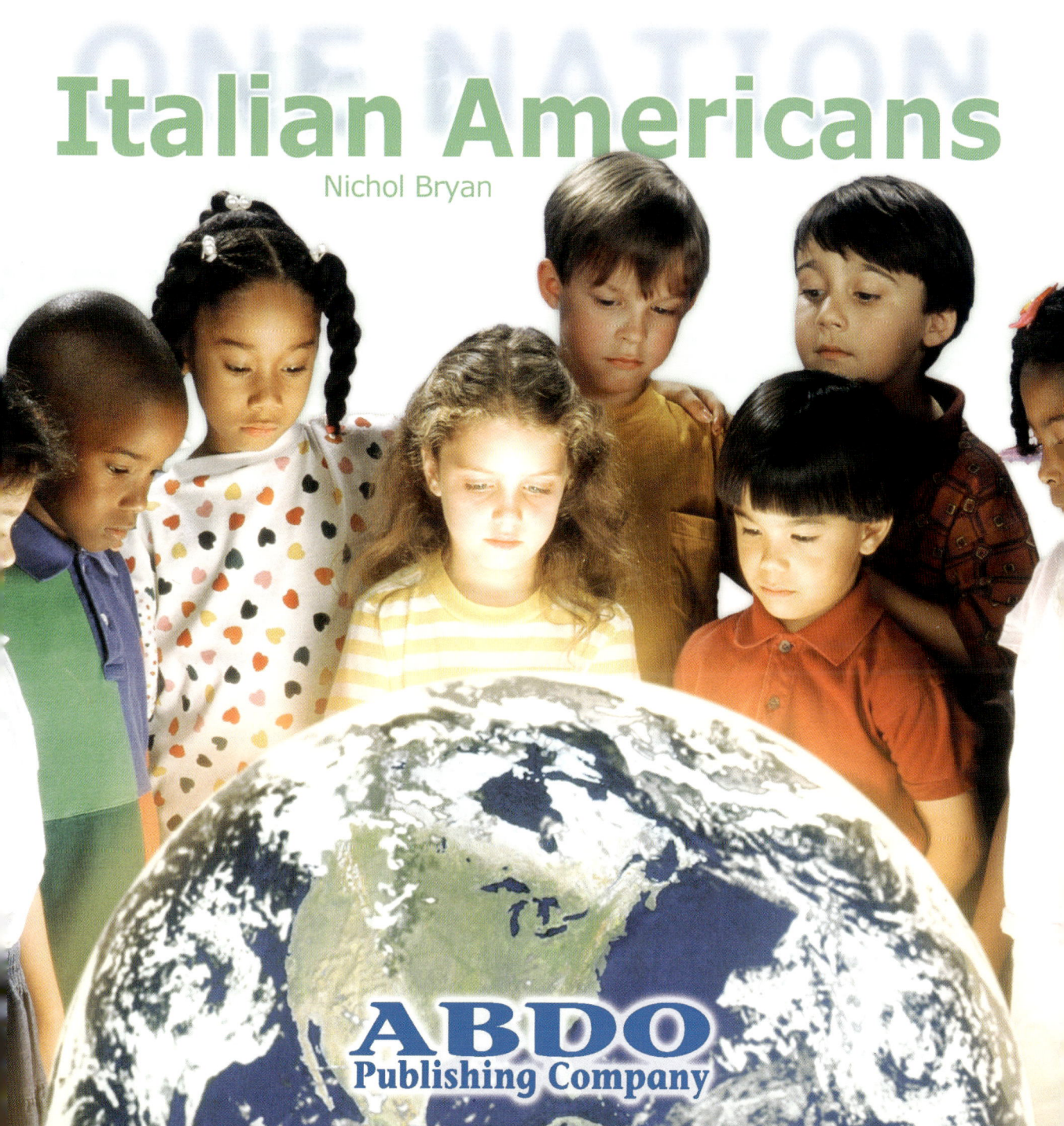

ONE NATION

# Italian Americans

Nichol Bryan

**ABDO**
Publishing Company

# visit us at
# www.abdopub.com

Published by ABDO Publishing Company, 4940 Viking Drive, Edina, Minnesota 55435.
Copyright © 2004 by Abdo Consulting Group, Inc. International copyrights reserved in all countries. No part of this book may be reproduced in any form without written permission from the publisher.

Printed in the United States.

Cover Photo: Corbis
Interior Photos: Corbis pp. 1, 2-3, 4, 5, 6, 7, 8, 11, 12, 15, 19, 21, 22, 23, 24, 25, 26, 27, 28, 29, 30-31

Editors: Kate A. Conley, Jennifer R. Krueger, Kristin Van Cleaf
Art Direction & Maps: Neil Klinepier

All of the U.S. population statistics in the One Nation series are taken from the 2000 Census. Special thanks to Carlotta Dradi Bower for help with the Italian language.

## Library of Congress Cataloging-in-Publication Data

Bryan, Nichol, 1958-
    Italian Americans / Nichol Bryan.
        p. cm. -- (One nation)
    Includes index.
    Summary: Provides information on the history of Italy and on the customs, language, religion, and experiences of Italian Americans.
    ISBN 1-57765-985-6
     1. Italian Americans--Juvenile literature. [1. Italian Americans. 2. Immigrants.] I. Title.

E184.I8B87 2003
973'.0451--dc21

2002043635

# Contents

# Italian Americans

How long have Italians been coming to the New World?  Ever since Christopher Columbus, an Italian explorer, landed there in 1492! In fact, the Americas were named after Amerigo Vespucci, another Italian explorer.

More than 500 years have passed since Columbus's landing. Since that time, millions of people from all over the world have decided to make the United States of America their home.  Many of these **immigrants** came from Italy.

Like other immigrants, Italians came to find a better life.  Some of them came to escape unfair treatment and war.  All of them brought their colorful **culture** and way of life to the United States.

*Amerigo Vespucci*

Life was not easy for the first Italian **immigrants**.  They faced **discrimination** and fear from other Americans.  Italian Americans struggled to overcome this.  Over time, they succeeded and have given back to America in many ways.

CHRISTOFLE COLOMB , GENEVOIS
Chapitre 100.

*A portrait of Christopher Columbus from the 1500s*

# A Long History

Italy is a European country shaped like a boot. It sticks out into the Mediterranean Sea. Italy has many mountains, and some of them are volcanoes. It also has fertile valleys and coastal plains. Italy's land includes many islands such as Sicily, which is an island at the tip of the boot.

Italy holds an important place in world history. Rome, the country's capital, was once the center of a world empire. The Roman Empire ruled parts of Europe, Africa, and the Middle East for nearly 500 years. Then in A.D. 476, the Roman Empire fell for many reasons, including troubles with its **economy** and military.

*Leonardo da Vinci's La Gioconda, also called the Mona Lisa, is one of the greatest works of the Renaissance.*

Italy was also at the heart of the Renaissance. The Renaissance occurred between the 1300s and the 1600s. During this time, people took a new interest in art, **architecture**, music, philosophy, and science. To this day, the Renaissance is remembered as a bright period in the history of Italy and of the world.

*A village in the Italian Alps*

*Italian troops during World War I*

Italy also has a history of problems, however.  Wars and disagreements kept the country weak and divided in separate states, even after the Renaissance.  The area was sometimes ruled by Austria, France, or Spain.  During these times, life for the average person was uncertain.

Italy was united into one country in 1861.  But, the new country's **economy** was unstable, and jobs were scarce.  So, many Italians began leaving Italy in the late 1800s and early 1900s.  They were forced to leave their homeland just to survive.  They went wherever they could find work.

Conditions in Italy did get better for some in the early 1900s.  The economy was improving as Italy entered World War I in 1915.  Italy was on the winning side in World War I.  But, many Italians died in the war.  When the war finally ended, many Italians were out of work.  Economic hardship spread all over Europe in the 1930s.

Despite these hardships, Italian **immigration** to America slowed at this time.  This happened because the U.S. government had placed limits on the number of immigrants it would accept.  Many Italians remained in their country and hoped for the best.

Italy's troubles were not over, however. A **fascist dictator** named Benito Mussolini had taken control of Italy in 1922. He joined forces with Germany's Adolf Hitler in World War II. During the war, battles raged up and down the Italian **peninsula**. When the war ended in 1945, much of Italy lay in ruins.

Italy rebuilt its businesses and industry after the war. It also joined many worldwide organizations. Italy became a member of the **North Atlantic Treaty Organization** and the **European Union**. Today, Italy contributes armed forces to peacekeeping missions worldwide. It is also a member of the **United Nations**.

With about 57 million people, Italy has become more peaceful and prosperous. It has a strong **economy**, and life is easier for those who live there. For these reasons, few Italians **immigrate** to the United States anymore. But, that was not always the case!

*Opposite page: Italian children go through a hard Christmas during World War II.*

# Birds of Passage

Italians have been coming to America ever since Europeans first landed there. The biggest wave of Italian **immigrants** came to America in the late 1800s and early 1900s. This was a time of great poverty and hardship in Italy. Between 1880 and 1920, 4 million Italians came to the United States.

These immigrants arrived in America after a long, difficult journey across the Atlantic Ocean. Officials met the travelers at Ellis Island, an island near New York. There, immigrants had a medical exam. Many of them had gotten sick on their journey, and some were sent back to Italy. Others were allowed to stay.

*A family of Italian immigrants arrives at Ellis Island in 1905.*

Most Italian **immigrants** did not plan to stay for long.  They intended to get good jobs in the United States and send money home to their families in Italy.  When they made enough money, they would go home.  Named after migrating birds, these first Italian immigrants were known as "birds of passage."

## The Journey from Italy to the United States

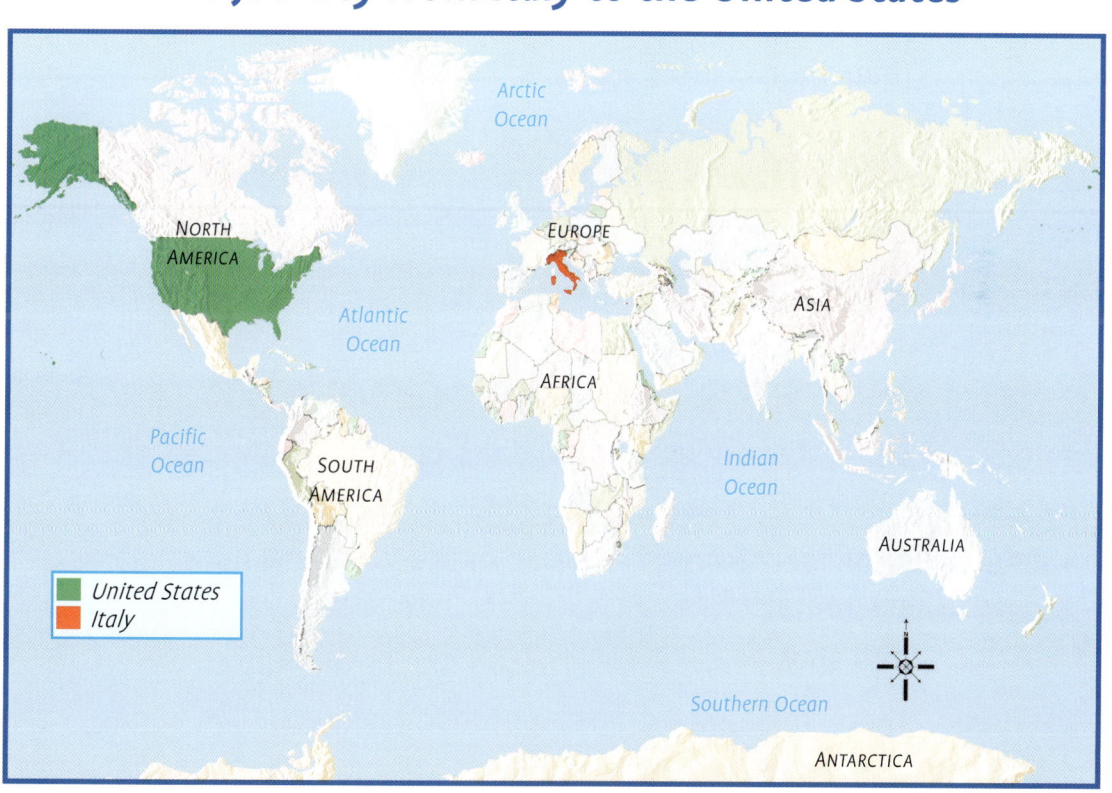

# New Americans

By the 1900s, more Italian families were coming to the United States to stay. They gathered in neighborhoods in cities such as New York and Chicago. The area in each city where they settled was later called Little Italy.

Perhaps the hardest part of American life for Italian **immigrants** was making a living. Most came to America with hardly any money. They had little education and spoke no English. Most of them had farmed small plots of land in Italy. They had no experience for the jobs they found in the United States.

The first Italian immigrants took whatever work they could find. Some went as far as Minnesota and Idaho to work in mining. The men worked in construction or as street cleaners in the cities. Italian-American women often worked in the garment industry, making clothes.

Other Italian Americans moved to the rich farmlands of California. There, they grew grapes and made wine. Italian wines

*Mulberry Street, a famous street in New York City's Little Italy, around 1900*

have been world famous since the days of ancient Rome. Italian-American wine growers with names like Gallo and Sebastiani brought this know-how with them. Thanks to these early Italian growers, California now produces some of the world's best wines.

Not all parts of Italian-American life were so bright. In fact, Italians often faced **discrimination** in America. The large number of Italians who **immigrated** to the United States shocked long-time residents. They feared that cities would be swamped with immigrants. Some thought the newcomers had strange, old-world ways.

In addition, most Italian immigrants were Roman Catholic. This made it harder for them to fit in with their neighbors, who were often Protestant. Many Americans also worried that Italians were **socialists**. That's because there was an important Socialist party in Italy. For these reasons, many Italians had a hard time living outside of the Little Italy neighborhoods.  They were kept out of better jobs and out of public office for many years.

Italian Americans faced new worries during World War II.  In the war, Italy fought against the United States.  Some people thought Italian Americans might be loyal to Italy rather than to America.  But, more than 500,000 Italian Americans fought in the U.S. armed forces during World War II.  They helped change people's minds about the loyalties of Italian **immigrants**.

Italian Americans also struggled with **stereotypes** in their new home.  In Italy, especially Sicily, there was an organized group of criminals called the Mafia.  Some Italians recreated the Mafia in the United States.  Some people started to think all Italian Americans were involved in crime, though most followed the law.  Italian Americans face this stereotype even today.

Italian Americans worked hard to overcome all these barriers.  They organized unions to gain better treatment at work.  The second generation of Italian Americans had an easier time being elected as mayors, city council members, and governors.  Italian-American business owners prospered, and conditions for the average worker improved.

As the experiences of Italian Americans began to change, so did America.  The Little Italy areas in the United States are still homes of Italian **culture**. However, most Italian Americans no longer live in isolated areas of cities. Italian Americans have found a place in every part of American society.

## Italian-American Communities

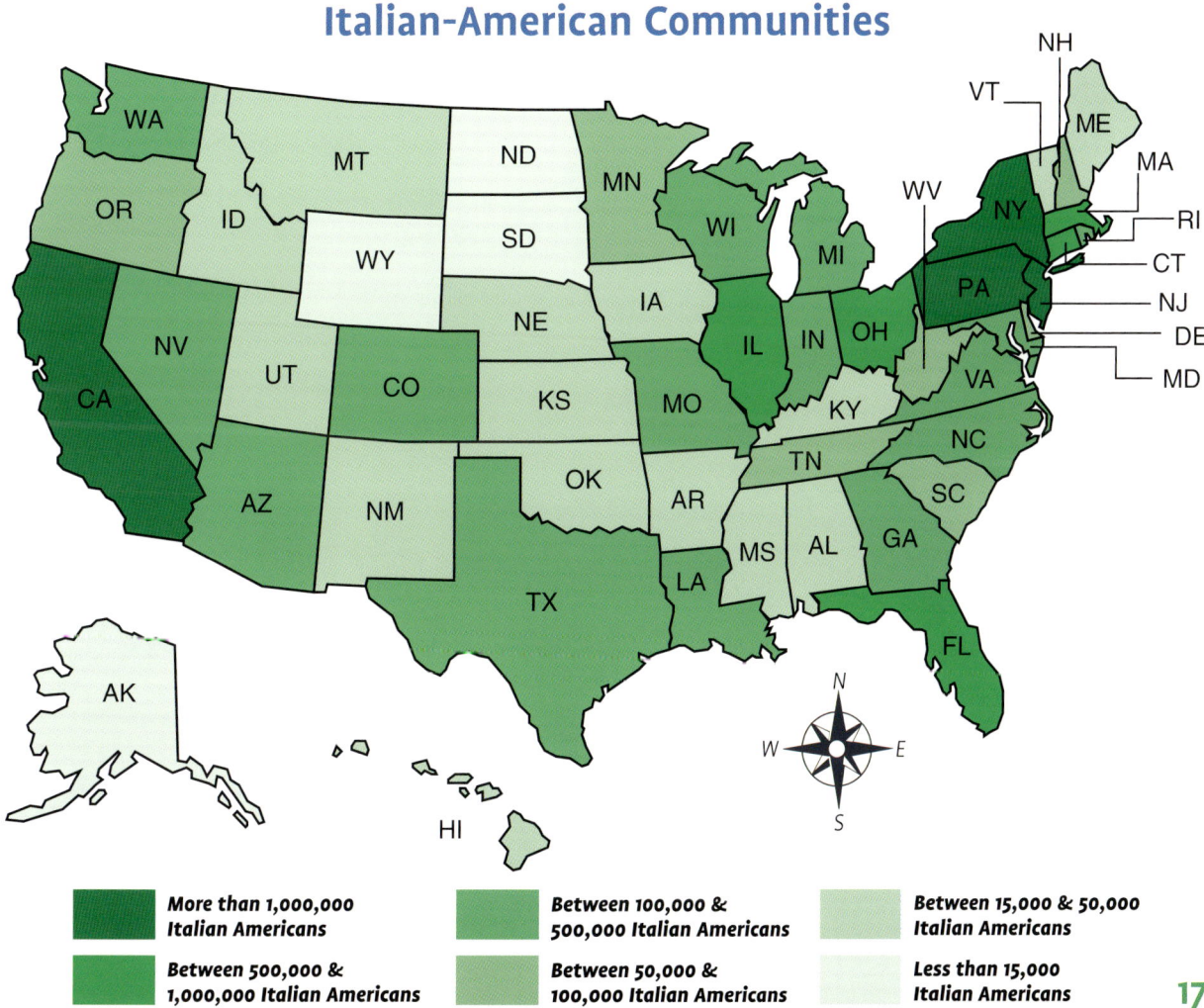

| | | |
|---|---|---|
| **More than 1,000,000 Italian Americans** | **Between 100,000 & 500,000 Italian Americans** | **Between 15,000 & 50,000 Italian Americans** |
| **Between 500,000 & 1,000,000 Italian Americans** | **Between 50,000 & 100,000 Italian Americans** | **Less than 15,000 Italian Americans** |

# Becoming a Citizen

Italians and other **immigrants** who come to the United States take the same path to citizenship. Immigrants become citizens in a process called naturalization. A government agency called the Immigration and Naturalization Service (INS) oversees this process.

## The Path to Citizenship

### Applying for Citizenship

The first step in becoming a citizen is filling out a form. It is called the Application for Naturalization. On the application, immigrants provide information about their past. Immigrants send the application to the INS.

### Providing Information

Besides the application, immigrants must provide the INS with other items. They may include documents such as marriage licenses or old tax returns. Immigrants must also provide photographs and fingerprints. They are used for identification. The fingerprints are also used to check whether immigrants have committed crimes in the past.

### The Interview

Next, an INS officer interviews each immigrant to discuss his or her application and background. In addition, the INS officer tests the immigrant's ability to speak, read, and write in English. The officer also tests the immigrant's knowledge of American civics.

### The Oath

Immigrants approved for citizenship must take the Oath of Allegiance. Once immigrants take this oath, they are citizens. During the oath, immigrants promise to renounce loyalty to their native country, to support the U.S. Constitution, and to serve and defend the United States when needed.

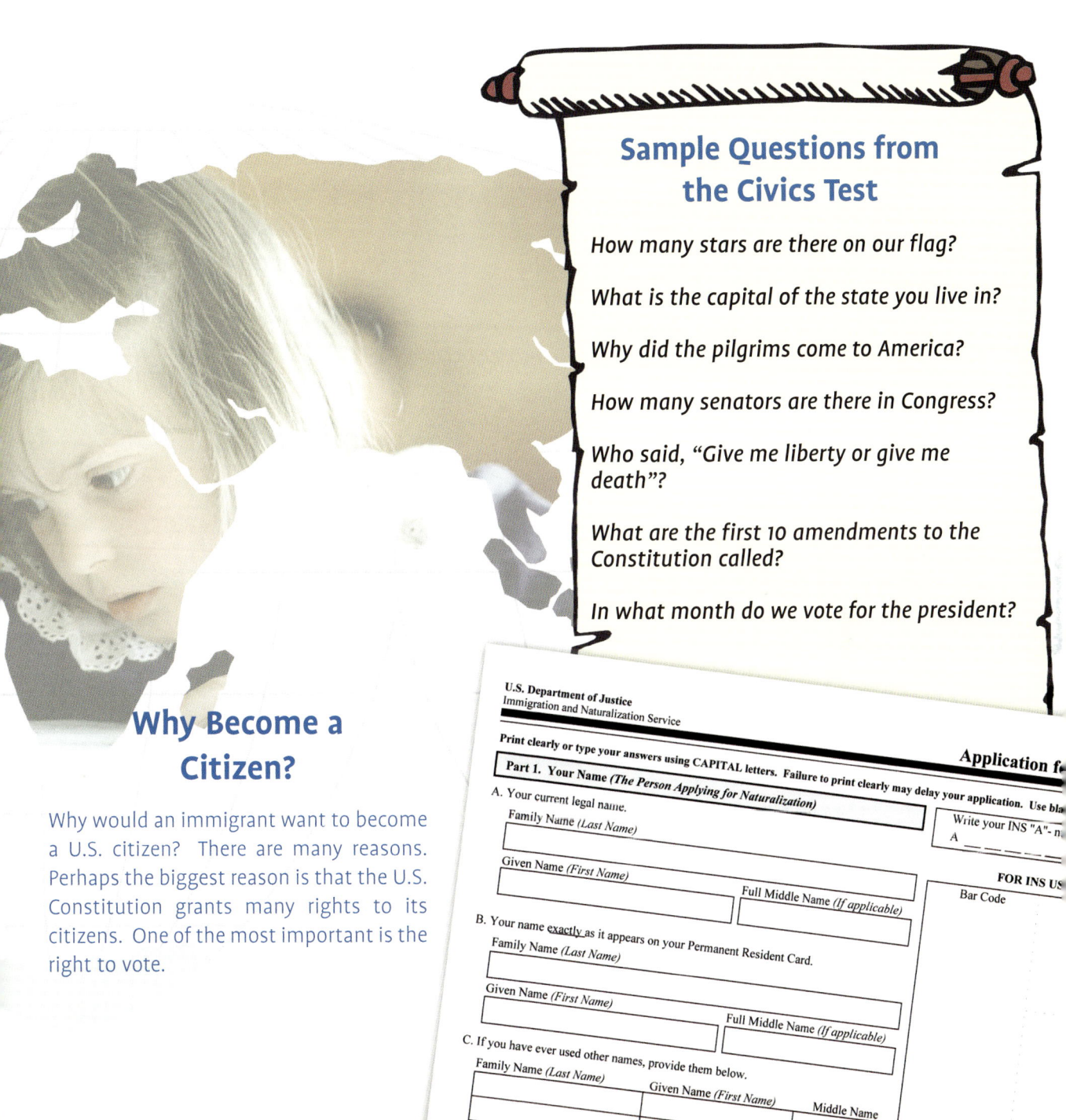

## Sample Questions from the Civics Test

*How many stars are there on our flag?*

*What is the capital of the state you live in?*

*Why did the pilgrims come to America?*

*How many senators are there in Congress?*

*Who said, "Give me liberty or give me death"?*

*What are the first 10 amendments to the Constitution called?*

*In what month do we vote for the president?*

## Why Become a Citizen?

Why would an immigrant want to become a U.S. citizen? There are many reasons. Perhaps the biggest reason is that the U.S. Constitution grants many rights to its citizens. One of the most important is the right to vote.

U.S. Department of Justice
Immigration and Naturalization Service

Print clearly or type your answers using CAPITAL letters. Failure to print clearly may delay your application. Use bla

**Application fe**

**Part 1. Your Name** *(The Person Applying for Naturalization)*

A. Your current legal name.

Family Name *(Last Name)*

Write your INS "A"- n

A

Given Name *(First Name)*

Full Middle Name *(If applicable)*

**FOR INS US**

Bar Code

B. Your name exactly as it appears on your Permanent Resident Card.

Family Name *(Last Name)*

Given Name *(First Name)*

Full Middle Name *(If applicable)*

C. If you have ever used other names, provide them below.

Family Name *(Last Name)*

Given Name *(First Name)*

Middle Name

# Way of Life

Even as Italian Americans blended into American society, they held on to their **culture** and history.  Italian traditions are played out every day in Italian-American families.  The contributions of Italian Americans to American life can be seen in their food, festivals, religion, and language.

## Family Comes First

For Italians, family is one of the most important parts of life. Traditionally, the father of an Italian family was expected to earn money.  The mother was expected to take care of the home and the children.

Today, most Italian-American families are like other American families.  Mothers have a more equal place in the family, having the choice to work outside of the home to earn money, as well.  And, children are more independent.  But, Italian-American families are still close.

Italian-American families such as this one are an important part of American culture.

# *Flavorful Foods*

Italian dishes have become everyday American food. But, did you know that many Italians in Italy ate pasta only on special occasions? After working awhile in America, they could afford to eat pasta more often than they could in Italy.

Today, Americans everywhere eat ravioli, lasagna, other noodles and pastas, tomato sauce, and homemade bread. These foods are all influenced by Italian cooking. Food is just one of the many ways Italian Americans have contributed to American **culture**.

*Spaghetti is an important part of many Italian-American dishes.*

# Festivals

Italian gatherings called festivals bring Italian Americans together all across the country. For the first Italian **immigrants**, the most important part of a festival was the parade where a certain saint was honored.

Which saint was honored depended on where and when the festival was held. A statue of the honored saint was paraded through the streets. Italians, some dressed in costumes from the Old Country, followed the statue along the parade route.

*The Feast of San Gennaro in New York City honors the patron saint of Naples, Italy.*

Today, a parade may be one part of a longer, carnival-like celebration that is the modern Italian festival. Italian food, music, and wine bring together members of the Italian community just as the original festivals did.

# A People of Faith

The Roman Catholic Church began in Rome nearly 2,000 years ago. Since then, the Catholic Church has had an important role in history.

Most Italians are Catholic, and their faith is an important part of their **culture**. When Italians **immigrated** to America, they brought this faith and culture with them.

*Children wearing religious costumes for a parade in an Italian-American festival*

The first Italian immigrants found only Irish Catholic churches in America. At these churches, the priests knew neither the Italian language nor Italian customs. So, Italians built their own churches where their traditions could be preserved. Of course, not all Italian Americans are Catholics. Some have joined other religions, while others follow no religious faith.

# The Italian Language

Some of the first Italian **immigrants** never learned English! Almost everyone in the community spoke Italian. Some Italian-American children were not even allowed to speak English at home. Most children, however, learned English at school.

Today, many Italian words are familiar to English speakers. For example, Americans use the Italian word *graffiti* to describe the writing and art people leave on public walls. Have you ever heard people use the word *ciao* to say goodbye? They're using another Italian word!

*The Italian language comes from Latin, a language from which English has borrowed many words. The Latin phrase e pluribus unum, which means "one out of many," can be found on many American coins today.*

# Cultural Gifts

Italian **immigrants** brought their love of the arts with them to the United States. In fact, the Capitol Building in Washington, D.C., owes much of its beauty to Italian Americans. Sculptors Enrico Causici, Antonio Capellano, and Luigi Persico worked to decorate the Capitol in 1805. Constantino Brumidi, another Italian American, painted designs inside the Capitol's dome.

Italian Americans made their mark in the world of music, too. One of the greatest Italian-American musicians was Arturo Toscanini. He was born in Italy and studied music there. Toscanini moved to the United States to escape **fascism** in Italy. He conducted many

*An illustration of Arturo Toscanini conducting in 1946*

**orchestras**, including the New York Philharmonic Symphony Orchestra and the NBC Symphony Orchestra. Through radio, Toscanini introduced millions of Americans to classical music.

Frank Sinatra, however, is perhaps the most famous Italian-American musician. The son of Italian **immigrants**, Sinatra grew up in Hoboken, New Jersey. He became a major singing star in the 1930s and 1940s. He went on to act in movies. Sinatra continued to record and perform hit songs for almost 60 years. His recordings of "New York, New York" and "My Way" are still popular.

Frank Sinatra

Italian Americans have also made a major impact on the world of film. Directors such as Francis Ford Coppola and Martin Scorsese, who is Sicilian, have made many award-winning and popular movies. For example, Coppola

**Francis Ford Coppola**

directed the *Godfather* trilogy, and Scorsese directed *Gangs of New York*. Scorsese also wrote and directed *My Voyage to Italy*, a movie about the history of Italian film.

One of the most famous Italian Americans, however, came from the world of sports. Joe DiMaggio played baseball with the New York Yankees in the 1930s and 1940s. He helped his team win the World Series nine times! He also served in World War II, missing some baseball seasons to serve his country. Joe DiMaggio is considered one of the greatest baseball players of all time.

Italian Americans also have a long history in U.S. politics. In fact, two Italian Americans, William Paca and Caesar Rodney, signed the Declaration of Independence. More recently, Rudolph Giuliani served as New York City's mayor from 1993 to 2001. Mayor Giuliani made the city safer by

**Joe DiMaggio**

reducing crime. He also received praise for his leadership when **terrorists** attacked New York City's World Trade Center buildings in 2001.

Other Italian-American leaders include Geraldine Ferraro, whose parents were Italian **immigrants**. In 1984, she became the first woman nominated by a major party to run for vice president of the United States. Antonin Scalia is another Italian-American leader. He is a member of the U.S. Supreme Court. Scalia's father was from Sicily, and his mother was also Italian American.

*Rudolph Giuliani*

Italian Americans have also become great inventors. For example, it is widely believed that Antonio Meucci, an Italian American, invented the telephone in 1871. That was five years before Alexander Graham Bell filed a patent for the telephone. Meucci had been too poor to pay the fee to file a patent, and he died in poverty.

These are only a few of the many Italian Americans who deserve recognition for their work. These creative, hard-working people did more than succeed in American society. They helped make America what it is today.

# Glossary

**architecture** - the art of planning and designing buildings.

**culture** - the customs, arts, and tools of a nation or people at a certain time.

**dictator** - a ruler with complete control who usually governs in an unfair way.

**discrimination** - unfair treatment based on factors such as a person's race, religion, or gender.

**economy** - the way a nation uses its money, goods, and natural resources.

**European Union** - an organization of European countries that works toward political, economic, governmental, and social unity.

**fascist** - of a political philosophy that favors a dictatorship and places nation or race above individual rights.

**immigration** - entry into another country to live.  A person who immigrates is called an immigrant.

**North Atlantic Treaty Organization** - a group formed by the United States, Canada, and some European countries in 1949.  It tries to create peace among its nations and protect them from common enemies.

**orchestra** - a large group of musicians playing mostly string instruments.

**peninsula** - land that sticks out into water and is connected to a larger landmass.

**socialist** - a person who believes in an economy where the government or the citizens control the production and distribution of goods.

**stereotype** - an oversimplified image of someone or something.

**terrorist** - a person who uses violence to threaten people or governments.

**United Nations** - a group of nations formed in 1945.  Its goals are peace, human rights, security, and social and economic development.

# Saying It

**Amerigo Vespucci** - ahm-ay-REE-goh vay-SPOOT-chee
**Antonin Scalia** - AN-tuh-nin skah-LEE-uh
**Antonio Capellano** - ahn-TOH-nee-oh cah-pehl-AH-noh
**Antonio Meucci** - ahn-TOH-nee-oh MAY-ooh-chee
**Arturo Toscanini** - ahr-TOO-roh toh-skah-NEE-nee
**Benito Mussolini** - beh-NEE-toh moos-soh-LEE-nee
**ciao** - CHOW
**Constantino Brumidi** - cohn-stahn-TEE-noh BROO-mee-dee
**Enrico Causici** - ehn-REE-coh COW-zih-chee
**Joe DiMaggio** - JOH duh-MAH-zhee-oh
**Leonardo da Vinci** - lay-oh-NAHR-doh dah VEEN-chee
**Luigi Persico** - looh-EE-gee PEHR-sih-coh
**Martin Scorsese** - MAHRT-uhn skaur-SEHS-ee
**Rudolph Giuliani** - ROO-dahlf joo-lee-AHN-ee
**Sebastiani** - SAY-bah-stee-ah-nee

# Web Sites

To learn more about Italian Americans, visit ABDO Publishing Company on the World Wide Web at **www.abdopub.com**. Web sites about Italian Americans are featured on our Book Links page. These links are routinely monitored and updated to provide the most current information available.

# Index